ALLISON STARK DRAPER

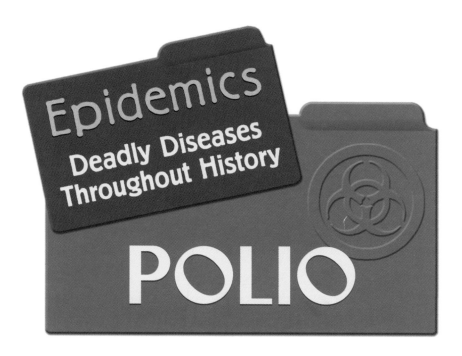

Epidemics
Deadly Diseases
Throughout History

POLIO

The Rosen Publishing Group, Inc.
New York

Published in 2001 by The Rosen Publishing Group, Inc.
29 East 21st Street, New York, NY 10010

Copyright © 2001 by The Rosen Publishing Group, Inc.
First Edition

Library of Congress Cataloging-in-Publication Data

Draper, Allison Stark.
   Polio / by Allison Draper—1st ed.
       p. cm. — (Epidemics!)
Includes bibliographical references and index.
   ISBN 0-8239-3348-2
   1. Poliomyelitis—History—Juvenile literature. 2. Poliomyelitis—New York (State)—History—Juvenile literature. [1. Poliomyelitis—History. 2. Diseases—History. 3. Epidemics—History.]
I. Title. II. Series.
   RC180.1. .D73 2000
   616.8′35′009—dc21
                                                    00-009371

Cover image: An electron micrograph of numerous virus particles (called virions) of the polio virus, which causes poliomyelitis.

Manufactured in the United States of America

CONTENTS

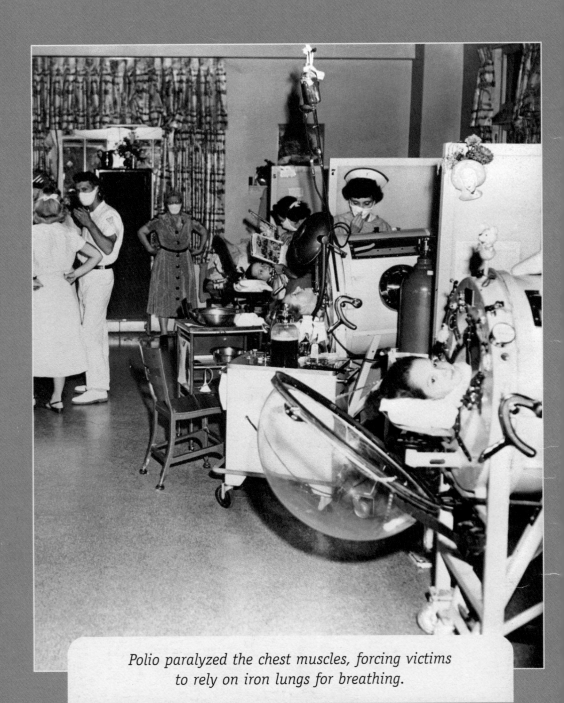

Polio paralyzed the chest muscles, forcing victims to rely on iron lungs for breathing.

INTRODUCTION

Polio, or poliomyelitis, has existed since the ancient days of human history. In the Carlsberg Museum in Copenhagen, Denmark, there is a carved stone plaque from the time of the New Kingdom Period of Egypt circa 1300 BC. It shows a man with a withered right leg and a dangling foot. He stands with the help of a cane. It is very likely that the man was a survivor of polio.

One of the first recorded cases of polio is that of Sir Walter Scott, the Scottish author of such adventure books as *Waverley* and *Ivanhoe*. Scott was born in Edinburgh, Scotland, in 1771. As a child, he suffered an attack of fever that lasted for three days. When it ended, he was unable to use his right leg. He had always been active and athletic. He found paralysis unbearable. He struggled against the weakness in his leg and walked long distances outdoors, at first dragging, and then slowly restrengthening his leg. In time, he regained his health and was even able to run and jump again.

The word "poliomyelitis" comes from the Greek words *polios*, which means "gray," and *myelos*, which means "matter." Gray matter is the nerve material found in the brain and spinal cord, the central nervous system (CNS). The CNS is responsible for controlling muscular functions in your body by relaying messages from your brain to your muscles. It allows you to move your body. If your CNS is damaged, you loose the ability to move or easily control the parts of your body that are connected to and controlled by that damaged nerve tissue. Sometimes when this happens, you are left totally unable to move the effected parts of your body. Those parts are paralyzed. Other times, people's limbs become only partially paralyzed which causes them to shrivel from lack of use and become deformed.

Polio is a virus that attacks the CNS. It has also been called infantile paralysis, because it most frequently affects children, or paralysis of the morning, because paralysis generally sets in overnight and people experience it in the morning. People who contract polio often go to sleep feeling only mildly ill but wake up to find that they are unable to walk, move one of their arms, or breathe without great difficulty. In fact, people whose chest muscles become paralyzed can lose the ability to breathe, which is one reason why people die from polio. If it is caught early on, these people can survive polio, but they often need a machine called an iron lung to help them breathe. The iron lung is a large tank that fits around the upper body of a patient. It is sealed at the neck with a rubber collar that stops air from escaping. Air is pumped into the tank and then sucked back out. This makes the patient's lungs expand and contract. The machine breathes for the patient, performing the activity that a healthy person's chest performs to push air in and out of the lungs.

When polio started breaking out in epidemic proportions, it was especially terrifying because its effects are so visibly horrible—people on crutches or in wheelchairs, people with shrunken limbs, people hooked up to iron lungs—and because doctors and scientists had so little information about the disease. They did not understand at that time what it was, how it worked, or how it traveled from person to person.

In the early 1900s, polio was one of the most dangerous diseases in the developed world. It spread fast, there was no cure, and victims would be crippled for life or would die.

1

A HISTORY OF POLIO

In 1789, an English doctor named Michael Underwood recognized and described a still-unnamed disease. He noticed that it occurred less often in London—a big, dirty city without plumbing—than it did in the countryside. By the mid-1800s, there had been so many cases that doctors started to investigate. A German doctor named Jacob von Heine thought the fact that the disease started with a fever might mean it was contagious—that it could be spread from person to person as opposed to being a disease that developed inside the body, like cancer. Heine worked with numerous cases and thought the disease should be treated with exercise and baths. He taught his patients to use braces to support their weakened limbs and help themselves learn to walk again. For the next 160 years, until the discovery of a vaccine, the methods of treating polio changed very little from those used by Heine.

In 1887, a Swedish doctor named Karl Oskar Medin saw that there were different forms of the disease. He recognized that the attack was made up of two fevers. The first fever was simply a fever, while the second attacked and damaged the central nervous system. In 1905, a Swedish children's doctor named Ivar Wickman dealt with an outbreak of more than 1,000 cases of the disease. He named it the Heine-Medin disease. In 1907, he investigated whether the disease was indeed contagious, as Heine had believed. If it was contagious, he

Polio sufferers often needed braces to support their weak arms and legs.

wanted to know how it spread. He wanted to find out whether children got sick only from direct contact with children who were already sick, or whether they could get sick from carriers—people who are infected but do not get sick or show signs of the disease. Carriers are dangerous because they unknowingly carry and spread disease to people who will get sick and suffer harmful symptoms. If people could be carriers of polio, Wickman reasoned, that would explain how polio could spread so quickly and so fatally even when everyone sick from it was usually separated from healthy people. Wickman thought that many, many people were carriers.

Epidemic!

During the early part of the twentieth century, polio epidemics suddenly became common. This did not mean everyone got sick or became paralyzed. The virus paralyzes only about 1 percent of the people it infects. (One percent may sound small, but that means that out of 1,000 infected people, ten will be paralyzed or will die.) Most people have asymptomatic infections—they are infected but show no signs of the disease. They are carriers. The virus enters their bodies, but they do not get sick. They do not even know that they have been infected with poliovirus. They carry the virus, but they do not realize that they are infected.

The reason polio is so dangerous and able to cause epidemics, is that it travels readily, under the right conditions, and can be passed easily from person to person. It is very contagious. It thrives in warm, urban

environments. Scientists also believe that it survives for a long time without a host or live organism, like a human, in which it can reproduce and grow. It is also not easily destroyed. Unfortunately, scientists did not have any of this information in 1916.

The New York Polio Epidemic of 1916

In the summer of 1916, there was a terrible outbreak of polio in New York City. Doctors diagnosed 9,000 cases. More than 2,300 people died. The people of New York were terrified. The outbreak started in an Italian neighborhood in Brooklyn. People immediately blamed the immigrants. The city government contacted the officials at Ellis Island, but they knew nothing. No immigrants had entered the United States who were already sick with polio. The officials at Ellis Island then contacted the Italian government to see if there had been any polio outbreaks in the towns and cities from which the immigrants had come, but there was no answer to be found there, either.

At that time, doctors still did not know how polio travels from one person to another, but they did know that many diseases live in dirt and garbage. The mayor ordered the streets of New York to be kept clean and that all garbage be disposed of properly and quickly.

1771
In Edinburgh, Scotland, first case of the disease later identified as polio is reported.

1789
English doctor Michael Underwood recognizes and describes the still unnamed disease.

1887
Swedish doctor Karl Oskar Medin further defines the disease.

1916
Polio epidemic breaks out in New York City. Doctors diagnose 9,000 cases and more than 2,300 people die.

And because quarantine—the removal of sick people from the general population—had worked to stop the spread of disease in the past, he forced the sick people into quarantine, either at home or in the hospital.

The quarantine regulations were incredibly strict. Parents who could not fulfill them at home had to send their children to the hospital; people who did not have enough space or money to create perfectly clean hospital conditions in a separate room in their home could not keep their children. The idea of sending a child to a polio ward full of sick children and strange nurses and doctors was terrifying. It was even scarier than trying to nurse a paralyzed child at home with no medicine and no experience. Some parents were so afraid to let

1926
Franklin Delano Roosevelt turns Warm Springs into a rehabilitation center for polio patients.

1940
Sister Elizabeth Kenny moves to the United States to treat polio patients.

1941
National Foundation for Infantile Paralysis (NFIP) officially endorses Kenny's methods to treat polio patients.

(continued)

their children go away that they hid them. If a family refused to send a sick child to the polio ward, the mayor sent police officers to take the child by force.

As drastic as these measures sound, this was the only hope that people had at the time for controlling this horrifying disease. People were convinced that these precautions would dramatically slow or even stop the spread of polio.

Searching for Answers

The authorities were desperate to understand the disease so they could be certain that the restrictions they were enforcing were actually the right way to

1951
Basil O'Connor hires Jonas Salk to create dead-virus polio vaccine.

1952
Salk tests newly developed vaccine at D. T. Watson Home for Crippled Children.

1954
Salk's polio vaccine tested on almost 2 million children. This was the largest medical experiment in history.

control it. They searched tirelessly for patterns. At one point, in July, they became convinced that African-American children did not get polio. In fact, as a weird extension of this idea, they suggested it was also possible that blond children caught it more easily than dark-haired children. But by August, the hospital wards were full of all types of children and it was clear that there was no difference in susceptibility between black children and white children—or among blondes, brunettes, or redheads.

Some people believed that the disease was carried by cats and dogs. Certain infectious diseases, such as rabies, are carried by animals and are deadly to human beings. Any explanation at all of how this terrible killer

1962	1999	2005
Albert Sabin's live-virus Oral Polio Vaccine (OPV) officially accepted by doctors.	Only 5,000 cases of polio reported worldwide as a result of rigorous efforts to vaccinate as many people as possible.	Tentative date for the worldwide eradication of polio.

spread was readily embraced by the people. It might be right and save the thousands of children who were not yet sick but who might be lost at any moment.

The people of New York started to kill every animal they could find. They captured and put to sleep both stray animals and their own pets. By the middle of July, people were killing between 300 and 400 animals a day. At the end of July, the *New York Times* announced that roughly 72,000 cats had died in the war on polio.

Second Guesses

As New York City got cleaner and cleaner, doctors started to recognize that polio might not be the result of a dirty environment. Polio was not more common in poor or dirty neighborhoods. It attacked every area of the city. It struck rich people and poor people, tidy people and messy people. But since they had no other answer, people refused to give up their conviction that perfect cleanliness would mean the end of the polio epidemic.

However, early in August, a comparison between the spread of polio on two New York City islands showed that dirt might really have nothing to do with the spread of polio. Barren Island in Jamaica Bay, Brooklyn, was one of the dirtiest places in New York. Barren Island was where the garbage barges took all of the garbage from every neighborhood in New York City. There were countless rats on Barren Island. There were flies, cockroaches, and mosquitoes. There was no public water system, no sewage system, and no garbage collection. There was also no polio. There were 350 children younger than sixteen years of age on Barren Island and not a single one of them had the disease.

The other island was Governor's Island. Governor's Island was owned by the military. It was clean and tidy. There was no polio among the 100 children on Governor's Island, either. A doctor in New York noticed this. He believed the lack of polio on both islands was due to isolation. The one thing the islands had in common was that the people living on

Children on Governor's Island were free from polio because they were isolated from the rest of the city.

them were separated from the people and the living conditions in the rest of New York. Because they did not come into contact with infected people or water supplies, or with objects that infected people had touched, the island dwellers had not come into contact with the disease.

The Aftermath

By the end of the 1916 epidemic, the United States public health officials had finally discovered some things about polio. They knew it traveled directly from one person to another—it was a contagious disease. They knew that it was not carried by animals or by insects—the way dogs carry rabies or mosquitoes carry malaria. They knew that many more people had it than got sick from it; most people who were infected were carriers. They suggested that in a major epidemic, like the one in New York City, many more people became carriers. These people were able to spread the disease unknowingly, and therefore posed a dangerous threat to the whole community. This knowledge was a step forward theoretically, but in practice only made scientists and doctors painfully aware there was almost nothing they could do to stop the disease from spreading.

2

TREATING THIS DISEASE OF DEVELOPMENT

Although polio has been around for thousands of years, it has done the most damage in the twentieth century. Polio is often referred to as a "disease of development." This means that the danger from polio has actually risen because of modern technology. Improvements in sanitation, like plumbing, protect people from contact with germs. But sometimes, exposure to germs allows your body to build defenses against the diseases they carry. Through coming into contact with a disease, your body builds an immunity by developing antibodies against that disease. When this happens, you become immune to that disease for the rest of your life. Polio is one such disease.

Before modern times, conditions were much more unsanitary. Almost every child came into contact with poliovirus as an infant. In very tiny children, polio infection is usually mild or asymptomatic. Children may have the virus in their bodies, but often they do not get sick. However, someone who encounters polio for the first time as an older child or adult is more likely to experience severe effects like paralysis or death.

At the end of the nineteenth century, most people in major cities in Europe and the United States had indoor plumbing. When indoor plumbing became common, most people were not exposed to poliovirus until they were older and more vulnerable to the harmful effects of the disease. They would often come into contact with the virus at school, where they encountered and played with other children who were infected, or by going swimming in a public pool in which infected people had swum.

The War on Polio: Franklin Delano Roosevelt and Basil O'Connor

Perhaps the most famous victim of polio is Franklin Delano Roosevelt, who served as president from 1933 to 1945. In 1921, when he was thirty-nine years old, he contracted the disease. Although tragic for Roosevelt personally, the disease did find a tough opponent in the future president. He was

President Franklin Delano Roosevelt contracted polio at thirty-nine.

wealthy, powerful, and determined to put an end to the disease. He declared a war on polio and established the National Foundation for Infantile Paralysis (NFIP). The NFIP declared it would not rest until it found a cure.

Roosevelt was paralyzed from the waist down after having suffered a fever for three days. But he was an athlete and a fighter. He refused to believe his paralysis was permanent. He was determined to regain the use of his legs. He found a spa in Georgia called Warm Springs, a place where people went to recover from various illnesses. He traveled there to see if bathing in the springs would help him.

Easing the Pain

Warm Springs is a group of mineral springs that is naturally heated by the earth to eighty or ninety degrees. Hot mineral baths are often prescribed for people with muscular pain. They help increase blood flow to the muscles and relieve pain due to lack of movement. Bathing at Warm Springs was ideal for a polio patient who had developed poor circulation and had trouble moving.

Roosevelt thought Warm Springs was a miracle for polio patients. In 1926, he decided to buy Warm Springs and turn it into a center for the rehabilitation

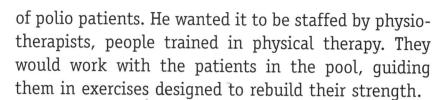

of polio patients. He wanted it to be staffed by physio-therapists, people trained in physical therapy. They would work with the patients in the pool, guiding them in exercises designed to rebuild their strength.

At this time, Roosevelt had a business partner, a lawyer named Basil O'Connor. When Roosevelt was elected governor of New York in 1928, he handed over the management of Warm Springs to O'Connor, who ran the spa with a savvy business sense and with passion. The fight against polio was also his fight. Not only was Roosevelt, who was one of his best friends, a victim, but so was his youngest daughter. Although his primary concern was to find a cure, O'Connor knew that, in the meantime, he needed to find an effective treatment to ease the pain of polio. Eventually he did, from an unex-pected and controversial source, Sister Kenny.

Sister Kenny

Because scientists who worked in the early part of the twentieth century had no real understanding of how polio works inside the body, doctors were unsure how to treat it. Most followed the age-old method of Heine, believing that paralyzed arms and legs should be immo-bilized. They used splints to force patients' limbs to stay straight. These splints were metal bars that were secured to the sides of a patient's legs with leather straps.

Elizabeth "Sister" Kenny believed that rebuilding muscles was crucial in the treatment of polio.

Not everyone agreed that this was the best way to treat paralysis. One person who disagreed was an Australian woman named Elizabeth Kenny. Kenny was born in 1880 and grew up on farms in New South Wales and Queensland. She became interested in medicine after breaking her wrist in a riding accident as a teenager. She first tested her medical knowledge on her younger brother Bill. She was convinced that his growth from a skinny boy into a vigorous man was the result of the exercises she made him do. Kenny trained as a nurse and worked in the Australian outback, fixing broken bones and delivering babies.

In 1911, Kenny was called to a farm to nurse a crippled two-year-old girl. Kenny had never seen any-

thing as awful as the disease that little girl had. It was polio, and there was no known cure. Nor was there any real treatment to ease the pain of the paralysis that many polio victims suffered. Kenny had to figure out what to do on her own. The first thing she noticed was that the girl's muscles were wasting away. She wrapped the girl's limbs in hot, wet rags, which later became known as Kenny's hot packs, and moved them to help rebuild the muscles the girl could not use herself. She believed the child's muscles had forgotten how to work and needed to relearn normal movement. When twenty more children in the area came down with polio, Kenny treated six of them, all of whom recovered completely.

Kenny served as a nurse in World War I. The soldiers called her Sister Kenny (because she was a nurse; not for religious reasons). Sister Kenny discovered that she had a gift for nursing under crisis conditions. After the war, she returned to the Australian outback but did not treat another polio patient until the 1930s. At this time in Australia, doctors like Jean Macnamara were defining the "real" medical treatment for polio, which followed along the same lines as those prescribed by Heine. Kenny thought Macnamara's belief in immobilization was a terrible mistake. She believed that because the splinted limb could not move easily, the muscles would disintegrate even more. Most doctors were more inclined to listen to Macnamara, who was a doctor, than to Sister Kenny, who was "only" a nurse and had no training in orthopedic medicine— the area of medicine that deals with bones and muscles. Then, during a polio epidemic in Melbourne, Kenny treated several severe cases, using her methods with great success. Two orthopedic surgeons took note of her work. Kenny gained a reputation for helping people doctors considered hopeless. Despite these successes, people still mistrusted Kenny's methods of treatment. Kenny's supporters thought she should take her ideas abroad. So in 1940, when she was fifty-nine years old, the Australian health ministry sent Kenny to the United States.

When Kenny arrived in the United States, many American doctors were following Dr. Macnamara's strategy of immobilization. They splinted and braced limbs or wrapped them in plaster casts. They were convinced that the sooner the limb was braced, the less likely it was to become twisted or deformed. Kenny began to fear she would find the same resistance in America that she had in Australia. At that time, there were a lot of polio cases in Minnesota. Kenny traveled to a hospital there and started working with patients and getting positive results. After some initial doubt, Kenny's results did finally speak

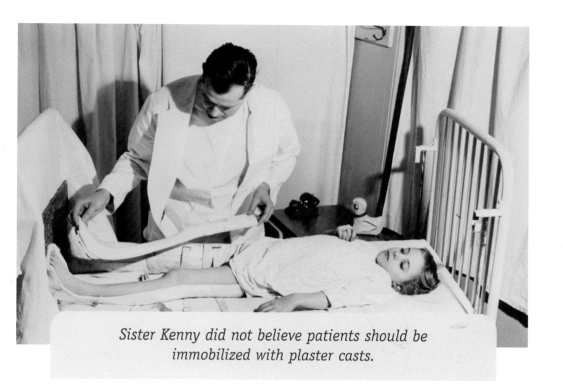

Sister Kenny did not believe patients should be immobilized with plaster casts.

for themselves. Doctors continued to criticize Kenny's lack of medical background, but patients and parents of polio victims loved her and so did O'Connor. He admired and supported Sister Elizabeth Kenny. And in December 1941, the NFIP officially endorsed her treatment methods and published a booklet describing her work. O'Connor—who had by then moved into the position of Chair of the NFIP, Treasurer of Warm Springs, and head of the American Red Cross—wrote the preface.

Sister Kenny had great faith in the strength and self-sufficiency of the patient. And she believed there was no need to use the cumbersome equipment on which so many doctors relied. She believed in reeducating patients and their muscles to stand and walk and run on their own. Unfortunately, Kenny's muscle theories could not solve all of the problems of polio. One piece of equipment that American doctors used, and that Kenny loathed,

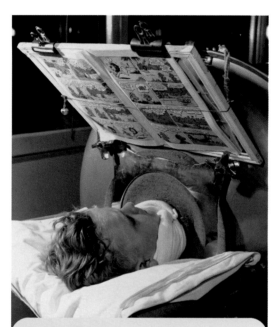

Sister Kenny hated seeing patients in the iron lung, but sometimes it was the only solution.

was the iron lung. In the same way that she objected to braces, Kenny objected to the machine. She saw it as an external solution that worked for the patient, allowing them to become weaker and more reliant on machines. She believed the patient needed to do the work alone. She believed only active recovery could restore full health. Sometimes Kenny removed patients from their iron lungs and, using hot packs and massage, helped them breathe again for themselves. But there were other patients that even Kenny had to admit would die without their iron lungs.

Unfortunately, Kenny's work—though tremendously important to so many sufferers—was only a treatment, not a cure, and it didn't work for everyone. There were many people who were still left crippled or dead. The disease was still in need of a cure.

Closing in on a Cure

By 1941, Franklin Roosevelt was president of the United States. World War II had begun and Roosevelt had other issues to concentrate on, so it was up to Basil O'Connor to take over the front line of attack in the war on polio. As a result of Roosevelt's diminished efforts, polio research lagged during the war. Then, in 1943, several British and American soldiers in Egypt came down with polio. The Egyptians believed that their country was polio-free before this outbreak. They suggested that the foreigners had brought the disease with them. In fact, there was polio in Egypt and had been for thousands of years. The difference was that, unlike in America or England, it was usually not fatal. Polio in Egypt tended to end in lameness or a withered arm rather than in severe paralysis or death.

Western doctors noticed that polio in the Philippines, in India, and in Malta behaved similarly to polio in Egypt. At this point researchers began to see the connection between cleanliness and polio. They realized that people who lived in cities and countries without indoor plumbing or organized trash removal were less likely to get sick from polio than people from England and the United States, where indoor plumbing and greater sanitation were more common.

With this discovery made, O'Connor assumed that the research might progress more quickly. He started looking for scientists who could lead the search for an answer. He found an anatomy professor named Dr. Harry Weaver. Weaver was smart, aggressive, and interested in working with O'Connor. O'Connor made him director of research. Weaver studied all of the research that had been done on polio. He came to a surprising and dramatic conclusion. He told O'Connor that he believed the only cure for polio was prevention. He said that people had to be stopped from getting the disease at all. Once it took hold of a person, there was no treatment that guaranteed full recovery. Polio patients could never fully undo their paralysis or fully regain the strength and use of their limbs. Weaver believed the only option was to invent a vaccine.

In order to work, a vaccine must protect people from every version of a virus. In the 1940s, researchers knew of three types or strains of polio-

For at least 2,000 years, people have known that someone who recovers from certain infectious diseases will not get sick from them a second time. This is the primary idea behind a vaccine. A vaccine is a little bit of a disease given to a person by a doctor. The person gets infected to a small degree, which raises the level of antibodies—the body's defense against disease—and once those antibodies have been produced, the person becomes immune to that disease. In order to make a vaccine safe, so that the patient will not actually contract the disease caused by the virus, the doctor weakens or kills the virus before injecting it. Even the weakened or dead virus is enough to help people raise their level of antibodies high enough to ensure immunity to the disease.

virus. Weaver told O'Connor that for the vaccine to be really effective, they had to know exactly how many types of poliovirus there were and what they were. Otherwise, everyone could be vaccinated and some unknown version of poliovirus could still make them sick. To figure out all the versions of the virus, scientists had to "type" it. This meant they had to compare every virus sample to the known virus strains to find out if there were more than the three they already knew about. This was incredibly boring work. Weaver knew they would need to test millions of samples, day after day, week after week, possibly for years. No important scientist wanted to sit in a lab and do this. Weaver decided to look for young, smart scientists who were not yet too important to do tedious work. One of the scientists he found was Dr. Jonas Salk, who would eventually create the first effective vaccine.

3

THE SCIENCE OF POLIO

Swedish pediatrician Ivar Wickman's ideas about polio turned out to be right—the disease was contagious and it was spread by carriers. This meant that it was probably caused either by bacteria or by a virus. At the time, medical researchers knew little about the differences between bacteria and viruses. They did know that viruses were smaller than bacteria. They could already stain bacteria with certain dyes and look at them under a microscope. A virus was too small to see under a microscope. (Today, scientists are able to look at viruses under electron microscopes, but the electron microscope was not invented until 1937.)

Bacteria or Virus?

Back in the early days of polio research, scientists could determine the presence of a virus only by seeing a person or a lab animal become sick from it. In 1908, two scientists in Vienna, Karl Landsteiner and Erwin Popper, took fluid from the spine of a polio victim. They put the fluid through a porcelain strainer. The holes in the porcelain were so tiny that it was not possible for any bacteria to pass through them. It was possible for a virus to pass through. Then they injected the filtered fluid into two monkeys. Both of the monkeys became sick with polio. This meant that polio had to be a virus. It also meant that polio could be defeated, as smallpox had been defeated, with a vaccine.

How Polio Spreads

Poliovirus travels from one host—the person in which the virus is living—to another via water or the surface of objects. It infects people who drink contaminated water or touch contaminated surfaces and then touch their mouth with their hands. Children are at great risk for infection because they tend to be more careless than adults about touching their mouth with dirty hands. Poliovirus enters and passes through the system

Bacteria are tiny organisms that live in the environment, in plants, and in animals such as human beings. Some bacteria are beneficial to humans, others are deadly. Bacterial diseases and infections in humans can often be treated with antibiotic medications like penicillin: "anti" means against and "biotic" means bacterial. Viral infections often look like bacterial infections, but they cannot be cured by antibiotics or other known medications. At this point, the only known weapon against a virus is vaccination. Viruses are different from bacteria in several important ways. Viruses are much smaller than bacteria and cannot be seen under a regular microscope but only under an electron microscope. They do not reproduce independently, like other organisms, but only copy themselves in the process of infecting another organism's cells, like those in a person. As a result, viruses are not exactly "living" organisms.

In 1935, two years before the discovery of the electron microscope, the first virus was isolated. Called the tobacco mosaic virus, this virus infected plants. Although they could not see the virus, scientists discovered that they could separate it from other material. Scientists isolated a sample of the tobacco virus and stored it for a long time without feeding it. They then put the virus onto a healthy tobacco plant. The plant immediately became sick. This meant that the virus had remained infectious without eating or reproducing. It did not age or change while in storage. This is not the way a living organism behaves.

of an infected person and is therefore present in human waste and in sewage. This makes it a fecal-oral infection. For example, if untreated sewage containing poliovirus enters a water source, a nonimmunized person who drinks the water can get sick.

There are places all over the world—including the United States—where sewage gets into rivers, lakes, and streams. For this reason, it is important never to drink water from an unknown source. Even in the wilderness, there is always the chance that a clear, clean-looking stream has been contaminated by impurities and disease. After a person is infected with poliovirus, it enters the stomach. From there it travels to the intestine. In the intestine, it burrows into the cells of the gut mucosa, or intestinal lining. It infects the cells and then replicates or makes copies of itself. Each time it replicates, it produces thousands of new virus particles, or virions, that can travel through the intestine and reach the sewage system to repeat the process. Often, the virus has no effect on the person it has infected. Other times it has a minor effect, making the person mildly sick but not dangerously ill. One percent of the time, poliovirus travels from the mucous lining of the intestine into the bloodstream. From here, it can invade the nervous system. It is only if it enters the central nervous system that polio can cause paralysis.

Clear water might not be as clean as it appears—it may be contaminated. For this reason, when you are outdoors, don't drink directly from rivers or streams.

Poliovirus operates on a microscopic level. When scientists say that it burrows into the intestinal lining, this means that a particle of poliovirus attaches itself to a single cell of the intestinal lining. The human body is made up of millions and millions of cells. A cell is so tiny that it can be viewed only under a microscope. Each cell in the human body has a nucleus in its center, which is the "brain" of the cell; a cell wall, which lets food into the cell and waste out of the cell; and proteins. When a particle of poliovirus reaches a cell, it attaches itself to a specific protein on the surface of the cell called a poliovirus receptor (PVR). The PVR creates a bridge

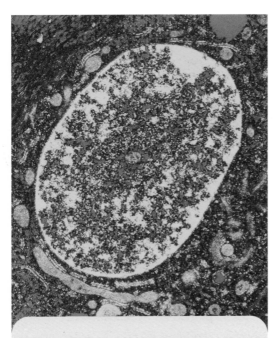

Each cell in the body has a nucleus, which controls the cell's functions.

between the inside and the outside of the cell. Poliovirus attaches to the PVR on the outside of the cell and then, when the PVR moves back inside the cell, the poliovirus tries to go in with it. This is a

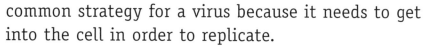

common strategy for a virus because it needs to get into the cell in order to replicate.

Viruses like polio are dangerous to cells because they destroy a cell's ability to function properly. Instead of doing its job maintaining the health of the body, the cell is taken over and turned into a virus factory. When the virus has replicated as much as it can in that cell, it shuts down the cell's own processes and waits for the cell to die. Then the cell dies or bursts in a process called lysis. The bursting releases all the new pieces of virus into the body. They find new healthy cells to infect, attaching to their PVR particles and widening the circle of infection.

Understanding Poliovirus Today

Despite the fact that polio has now been successfully conquered by a vaccine, scientists still do not completely understand how the virus spreads through the body. Some researchers think the virus travels through the bloodstream. Others think it is able to go directly to the nerves. In one experiment, scientists bred mice to be genetically susceptible to polio. This meant that every mouse would get sick. They injected each mouse in the left leg with poliovirus. The virus moved from the left leg to the spinal cord to replicate. Interestingly, even though the spinal cord is in the middle of the body, the left leg was still the first place to be paralyzed. The scientists then cut the nerves between the left leg and the spinal cord of some mice before they injected the virus. In these mice, the virus did not reach the spinal cord, even though there was still blood moving between the left leg and the spinal cord. This suggests that the virus travels through the nerves to reach the spinal cord and not through the blood. This is only a possibility, however. The fact that this is what happened in genetically engineered mice does not mean it is how a normal infection of polio works in a human being.

Regardless of how much information scientists and doctors uncover about how polio infects and spreads throughout the body, they still agree that the best solution to fighting the disease is vaccination.

4

PREVENTING POLIO: FINDING THE VACCINE

Dr. Jonas Salk was born in 1914 in New York City. He entered the City College of New York at age fifteen in 1929. When he graduated, he went to the New York University School of Medicine. In his first lecture, he learned that it was possible to immunize people against a disease using a chemically created toxin. In the second, he learned that it was necessary for a person to have some amount of a real disease, either as an illness or as a vaccination, in order to develop immunity to it. Salk was intrigued by these two discoveries. He felt sure that they could not both be true. He became intensely interested in immunology.

After New York University, Salk went to the University of Michigan where he worked with Dr.

Thomas Francis. Francis was working on a vaccine for influenza using dead, or inactivated, viruses. Salk started to learn about vaccines made with dead or inactivated viruses. From Michigan, Salk went to Pennsylvania where he began to pursue his own work. When Dr. Weaver called him to help with the polio project, Salk was very interested. Most of the people involved in polio work believed they needed to find a live-virus vaccine, in which a small amount of weakened or altered virus was used. But Salk believed it might be possible to create a dead-virus vaccine for polio.

In September of 1951, the NFIP organized the Second International Poliomyelitis Conference. They held it at the University of Copenhagen, Denmark. Salk went. He sailed there with Basil O'Connor on the *Queen Mary*. Salk was smart and funny, and O'Connor liked him. Many of the scientists O'Connor had met were interested only in what they did in the lab. Salk was interested in how science could help people. O'Connor wanted to find a cure for polio to help people, not because it was an interesting scientific problem. O'Connor and Salk became partners. O'Connor had the power and the money. Salk had scientific knowledge and vision.

In 1952, there were 58,000 new polio cases in the United States. Five thousand people died. Parents kept their children out of school. They avoided movie

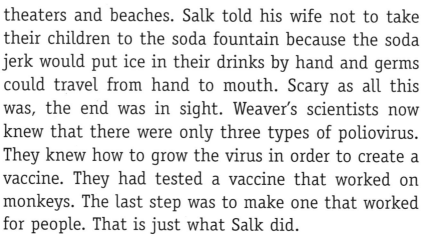

theaters and beaches. Salk told his wife not to take their children to the soda fountain because the soda jerk would put ice in their drinks by hand and germs could travel from hand to mouth. Scary as all this was, the end was in sight. Weaver's scientists now knew that there were only three types of poliovirus. They knew how to grow the virus in order to create a vaccine. They had tested a vaccine that worked on monkeys. The last step was to make one that worked for people. That is just what Salk did.

In the spring of 1952, Salk got permission from the medical director of the D. T. Watson Home for Crippled Children to do a test on the polio patients there. He would inject them with vaccines made of the version of poliovirus they already had. If it raised their antibody levels, he would know the vaccine was working. There was no danger—these people were already infected and would not get more sick—and if it worked, it would mean hope for an effective vaccine. The injections were a success. When Salk injected the patients, their antibody levels rose more than they had when the patients had actually contracted the disease. Salk then did a second test. He used the vaccine on a group from the Polk State School, none of whom had ever had polio. This time, the antibody levels rose in people who had never had the disease. Salk's vaccine was a success.

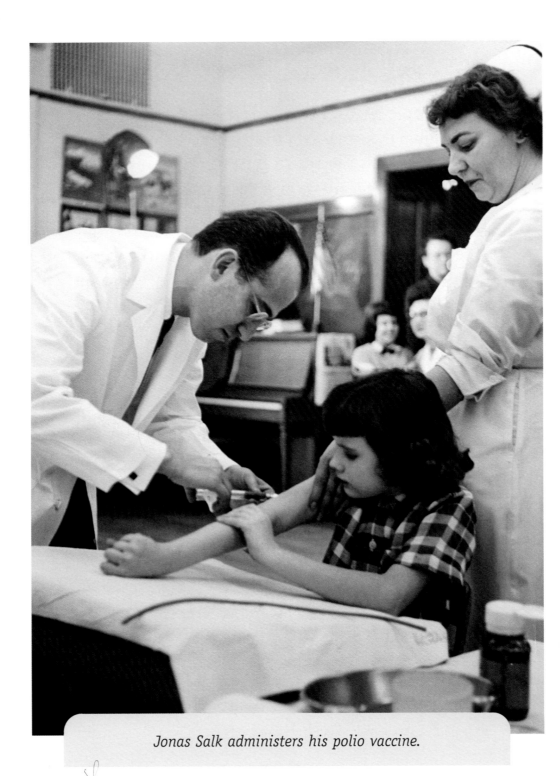

Jonas Salk administers his polio vaccine.

O'Connor was thrilled. The war on polio was nearly won. O'Connor organized the NFIP to put together a major field trial. They decided to test the vaccine on two million children. Some would receive the vaccine and some would receive placebos. A placebo looks and feels like the real vaccination but instead of the vaccine, the shot would contain only sugar water. The placebo group would think that they were receiving the vaccine, but they would not. This would ensure that any difference in antibody levels between the two groups would be due only to the vaccine and not to the excitement of the trial or some other factor the scientists had not taken into consideration. Every major scientific trial has a placebo or control group for this reason.

This vaccination project was an enormous undertaking. Tens of thousands of volunteers at NFIP offices all over the country helped organize the vaccine injections. Salk's goal was to test the vaccine on 1,800,000 children.

O'Connor never questioned that the vaccine would work. Before the test was over, he had spent 9 million dollars on 27 million doses of vaccine—the largest medical experiment in all of history. This undertaking was risky because O'Connor didn't actually have the money, and he would be able to get it only if the vaccine was a success. But he was confident, and his only priority was to make sure that as many children were protected from this awful disease as possible. It was chancy, but he could think of no worse situation than to have a successful vaccine and not have paid for enough to protect all the children who wanted it.

The test was a success, and the vaccine was officially pronounced safe, effective, and potent. More than fifty years of fear and suffering were ended. The American people went crazy. They had waited so long and suffered so much. They adored the quiet, intelligent Dr. Jonas Salk. The war on polio was finally over, and Salk was their hero. He immediately became a celebrity. He was frequently on television, his picture was on the front page of virtually every newspaper and on the cover of virtually every magazine.

The only people who were not excited were other scientists. They objected to the press conferences and magazine pieces that made Salk seem like a movie star. This was not how scientists behaved. The public assumed that these scientists were just jealous.

But there were real reasons to take issue with this method of vaccination. The primary objection the scientists had was that Salk's discovery of the polio vaccine was not a discovery at all; it was just an application of ideas that had been around for years. They also argued that the use of the dead-virus vaccine was perhaps not the best answer. It

was expensive—three separate injections were necessary. Also, the effects were only temporary—each shot would probably last for no more than a few years, which meant that a booster injection would be needed to revive its strength.

The scientists who made this argument believed that Salk's vaccine was inferior to a live vaccine. A live vaccine would offer permanent immunity. It would also be a scientific advance. There were other scientists who said that criticizing Salk was ridiculous. He had solved a problem that had deeply troubled the world for more than half a century. He had saved millions of lives. In the end, though Salk was adored by the public and was considered a success by most people's standards, he was never recognized as a pioneer by the scientific community. He was never nominated to the National Academy of Sciences and he never received the Nobel Prize, two honors that many believed he deserved.

Live-Virus Vaccine

The foremost live-virus vaccine scientist was Albert Sabin. Sabin was very critical of Salk. He, along with many other scientists, thought that Salk had failed as a scientist because he settled for the easy solution. He also thought that live-virus vaccines were the

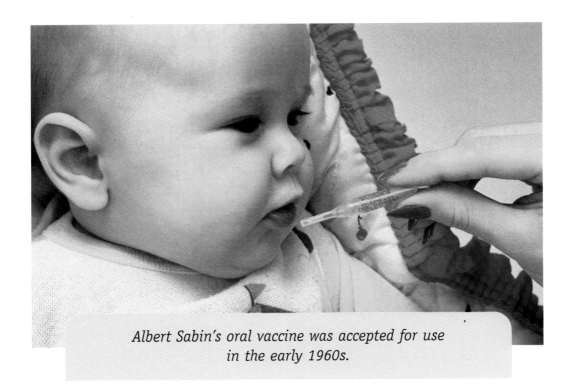

Albert Sabin's oral vaccine was accepted for use in the early 1960s.

immunological solutions of the future. Dead-virus vaccines seemed to him to be an old-fashioned short-term solution rather than real scientific progress. But the American public was not interested in what Albert Sabin thought. It was Jonas Salk who had freed them from the fear of polio. And the number of American lives Salk had saved grew daily. People out-side of the scientific community saw no need for another answer to the polio problem.

After Salk's success, there was little money and less public support for live-virus research. Sabin decided to go abroad. He went to England and, like Sister Kenny, found much more support in another country than he had in his own. Sabin finished his work and created a live-virus vaccine. In 1961, during a polio outbreak in Hull, England, he was able to use it. In October, Sabin began giving people his live-virus oral vaccination. Early in 1962, the Sabin Oral Polio Vaccine (OPV) was officially accepted by doctors.

5

ERADICATION: THE DEBATE CONTINUES

The debate over whether the dead- or the live-virus vaccine is better has caused great tension throughout the search for a polio vaccine. Clearly, the success of the Salk vaccine did not put an end to this controversy. Many scientists today still argue that the live-virus vaccine is superior.

The Salk vaccine is an injection of a small amount of actual poliovirus that has been killed in a lab using heat or chemicals. The injection teaches the human immune system to recognize and eliminate poliovirus. The vaccine makes people immune to polio for a long time, but not necessarily for their whole lives.

Live vaccine is made from poliovirus that is grown in a lab under a series of different conditions that force it to mutate or change. The weakened, or attenuated, virus that results from this mutation is given to a patient orally. The weakened virus can replicate in the intestine, but usually cannot grow strong enough to attack the central nervous system. Like Salk's vaccine, this is a way to teach the body to recognize the virus and become immune it.

Both vaccines have benefits and both have risks. One major advantage of the live vaccine is that unlike the Salk vaccine, which is an injection, it does not require a trained medical person to administer it. In addition, it is much less expensive, needs to be given only once, and offers life-long immunity. The disadvantage is that there is a slight (one in a million) risk of paralysis. To administer the Salk vaccine, a trained medical person is needed and the patient may be required to get a booster shot to maintain long-term immunity. However, there is zero risk of paralysis.

In a short time, the vaccines created by Sabin and Salk eradicated polio in most of the developed world. Today, in parts of the world where there is little money for health care, the less expensive Sabin vaccine is used. Because it is so cost effective, many people believe that it is the Sabin vaccine that makes eradication, or total elimination of polio, a real possibility.

AFRICA: THE DIFFICULTIES OF ERADICATING POLIO

The polio epidemic has been most difficult to control in Africa. In many countries, health care issues are overlooked because of political problems or war. In some cases, the wartime fighting makes it impossible for health workers to enter a country and vaccinate people. Sometimes health workers request a cease-fire, which is a time when armies agree to stop shooting. When a government at war agrees to a cease-fire, health workers are able to go in and vaccinate the people.

In the Democratic Republic of Congo in the 1990s, civil war made it impossible to deliver vaccine supplies. In 1995, there were more than 1,000 cases of paralytic polio in the city of Kisangani. A more hopeful story is that of Ethiopia. The Ethiopians have worked hard to eradicate polio. In 1998, they spent almost $6 million on a vaccination campaign. They hired 90,000 health-care workers to organize National Immunization Days. On these days, the workers set up at hospitals, clinics, schools, churches, mosques, and community centers. They vaccinated more than nine million children against polio.

In recent years, there have been only a few small outbreaks of polio in less developed countries. The problem is that the use of Sabin's live-virus vaccine means that everyone who is vaccinated is actually producing tiny amounts of live virus. This is because Sabin's vaccine actually is the poliovirus. It combines three mutant strains of polio that have the potential to mutate into a virulent or deadly form of the virus.

This means there may be dangerous viral material in the sewage systems of such polio-free countries as the United States.

There are samples of live poliovirus all over the world. Everyone who has ever studied polio has used real poliovirus, so there are polio samples in thousands of labs and hospitals. If one of these samples were set loose accidentally—or on purpose—it could start another epidemic.

Warfare with Polio

Another danger is biological terrorism. Biological terrorism is when one army or country infects the people they are fighting with a disease. There has been accidental biological terrorism throughout history. When the Europeans first arrived in America, they brought smallpox with them. Hundreds of thousands of Native Americans died in terrible epidemics. This helped the Europeans take over North and South America. When smallpox was eventually eradicated, there were just two samples of it left in the world. People worried they might be used by one country against another. Some people wanted to destroy the samples. Others said it was foolish to destroy any scientific knowledge. Destroying information is dangerous. One never knows what could be useful in the future.

POST-POLIO SYNDROME: THE DISEASE LINGERS

In the past decade, roughly 25 percent of survivors of acute cases of polio have reported a recurrence of symptoms similar to polio, although they no longer have the disease in their system. These may be symptoms of post-polio syndrome, or PPS.

Doctors do not yet understand the cause of PPS. They do know that during acute poliomyelitis, many motor nerve cells, which tell muscles what to do, die. The remaining cells need to send out new nerve terminals to command the muscles that have lost their own nerve cells. Based on this information there are four major theories to explain PPS.

1. Thirty or forty years after suffering from polio, the substitute nerve terminals may stop working.

2. The remaining original motor nerve cells may start dying after decades of working for so many extra muscles.

3. PPS could be an autoimmune problem. This means that the immune system (which is designed to fight off disease) of a PPS sufferer attacks the person's body.

4. Poliovirus may reactivate in the bodies of people with PPS. This seems unlikely because people with PPS are not able to infect others with polio.

The fact that so little is known about PPS makes it difficult to treat. It seems true that people who pushed themselves the hardest to regain their strength, like Sister Kenny's patients, are now suffering the most. Doctors usually recommend that sufferers slow down and treat themselves more gently. Unlike the war on polio, the war on PPS is not a fight against a disease; it is a battle for the continuing health and comfort of every polio survivor.

Polio is also a very durable virus. It can probably survive for long periods of time in water or soil, without a human host. The scary fact is that we do not know how long the virus can survive. It is possible that in areas where drinking water is recycled, the virus could survive indefinitely.

Getting Rid of Polio

If polio can be eliminated by vaccination, why isn't everyone vaccinated? World vaccination is expensive and labor-intensive. Health organizations want to reach a point at which the disease will be eradicated. They want to set a date by which vaccination, because it has done its job so well, will no longer be necessary. (Currently the date is set at 2005.) Unfortunately, it will be hard to know when to stop vaccinations or if the virus has actually been eliminated. Since the virus could be active for an indefinite period of time, any new generations that are not vaccinated would be at risk of contracting polio. Some people believe that it would be best to keep vaccinating indefinitely.

There are valid concerns about whether or not keeping the virus is safe. Polio is a perfect weapon for biological terrorism. It travels through water and food. It is extremely difficult to detect, and it is very contagious.

In a city of 10 million unvaccinated people, at least 7,000 would die in another polio epidemic. But this does not necessarily mean people should destroy all the existing poliovirus. It is also possible that if all the poliovirus in the world were destroyed, scientists could create more through the use of genetic technology.

The Future

The good news is that during the 1990s, the worldwide number of polio cases decreased by 90 percent. In 1999, only 5,000 cases were identified. Unfortunately, a permanent answer to polio may be more complicated than even the dead-virus versus live-virus vaccination question. One hope is that the lessons we have learned about fighting diseases from the war on polio will extend beyond polio. We can learn from the methods that have been successful and apply them to the fight against other infectious diseases like AIDS, tuberculosis, and malaria. Perhaps the real answer to polio and to all viruses involves technology that goes beyond the realm of vaccinations. Perhaps science will one day develop an immunological technology that will help in the human fight against all viruses. Perhaps the war on polio will become part of the larger human war on viruses, in which scientists continue to seek a new and more permanent victory over these mysterious diseases.

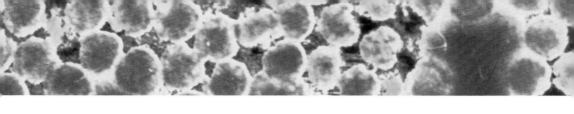

GLOSSARY

antibody   Substance in the body present or produced in response to infection.

asymptomatic   Showing no symptoms of a disease with which one is infected.

bacteria   Microscopic organisms that live in soil, water, or the live bodies of plants or animals; they can be either helpful or harmful to the body they inhabit.

brace   Pair of splints connected by leather straps that fastens at the sides of the leg to support weakened muscles.

carrier   Person who does not get sick from a disease but can pass it on to others.

contagious   Disease that can be passed from one person to another, or a stage of being infected in which one person can pass a disease to another person.

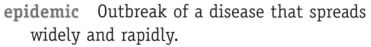

epidemic   Outbreak of a disease that spreads widely and rapidly.

genetic engineering   Changing or re-creating organisms by altering or copying genes.

host   The human or animal in which a virus lives.

immunity   Ability to resist a disease.

infection   Establishment of a sickness in a living organism.

iron lung   Machine that inflates and deflates the lungs of people with paralyzed chest muscles so they are able to breathe.

nervous system   The brain, nerves, and spinal cord.

paralysis   Complete loss of motion and feeling in a body part.

physiotherapist   Someone who treats disease physically, using massage, exercise, water, and heat.

placebo   Nonactive medicines that patients believe are real.

quarantine   To isolate people with a contagious disease so they cannot spread infection.

replicate   To copy or reproduce.

toxin   Poisonous substance.

unsanitary   Unclean.

vaccine   Injection, liquid, or pill that produces immunity to a particular disease.

virus   Submicroscopic infectious material that causes disease.

FOR MORE INFORMATION

In the United States

Centers for Disease Control (CDC)
1600 Clifton Road
Atlanta, GA 30333
(404) 639–3311
Web site: http://www.cdc.gov

World Health Organization (WHO)
525 23rd Street NW
Washington, DC 20037
(202) 974-3000
Web site: http://www.who.int

In Canada

Clinical Trials Research Centre
IWK Grace Health Center
5850 University Avenue
P. O. Box 3070
Halifax, NS B3J 369
(902) 428–8141
Web site: http://www.dal.ca/~ctrc

Property and Public Health Branch
Bureau of Infectious Diseases
Health Canada
Tunney's Pasture
Ottawa, ON K1A 0L2
(613) 957-2991
Web site: http://www.hc-sc.gc.ca

Web Sites

Polio Information Center Online
http://128.59.173.136/PICO/PICO.html

Post-Polio Syndrome
http://home.earthlink.net/~polioinfo/

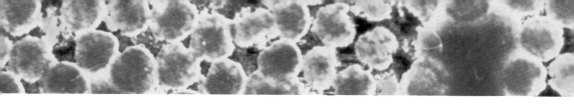

FOR FURTHER READING

Black, Kathryn. *In the Shadow of Polio*. Reading, MA: Addison Wesley Longman, Inc., 1997.

Gould, Tony. *A Summer Plague: Polio and Its Survivors*. New Haven, CT: Yale University Press, 1997.

Kehret, Peg. *Small Steps: The Year I Got Polio*. Morton Grove, IL; Albert Whitman & Co., 1996.

Mee, Charles L. *A Nearly Normal Life: A Memoir*. New York: Little, Brown & Co., 1999.

Seavey, Nina Gilden, Jane S. Smith, and Paul Wagner. *A Paralyzing Fear: The Triumph over Polio in America*. New York: TV Books, 1998.

Spies, Karen Bornemann. *Franklin D. Roosevelt*. Springfield, NJ: Enslow Publishers, Inc., 1999.

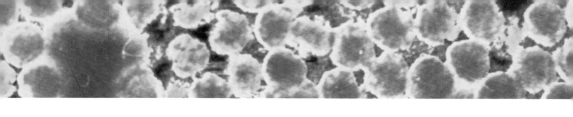

INDEX

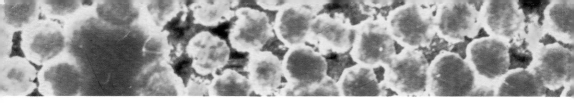

CREDITS

About the Author

Allison Stark Draper is a writer and editor. She lives in New York City and the Catskills.

Photo Credits

Cover photo by CNRI/Science Photo Library/Photo Researchers; pp. 4, 27, 44 © Bettman/CORBIS; p. 9 © Steve Raymer/CORBIS; p. 17 © Richard Drew/Associated Press AP; p. 21 © Associated Press FDR Library; p. 24 © CORBIS; p. 28 © Hulton-Deutsch Collection/CORBIS; p. 37 © Kevin Syms/Pictor; p. 38 © J.L. Carson/Custom Medical Stock Photo; p. 48 © Aaron Haupt/Photo Researchers.

Design and Layout

Evelyn Horovicz